IMAGES
of England

REDDISH

Joyce Brindley (née Allison), newly-crowned Rose queen of St Agnes' church, 1958. Joyce proceeds along Gorton Road near St Agnes' church and St Agnes' Street followed by her four train bearers, three maids-of-honour and two ladies-in-waiting. The No. 17 bus follows them advertising the football ground, Reddish, as its destination. The main road, still cobbled in those days, shows the marks where the tram lines have been filled in.

IMAGES
of England

REDDISH

Compiled by
Jill Cronin

TEMPUS

First published 2000
Copyright © Jill Cronin, 2000

Tempus Publishing Limited
The Mill, Brimscombe Port,
Stroud, Gloucestershire, GL5 2QG

ISBN 0 7524 1878 5

Typesetting and origination by
Tempus Publishing Limited
Printed in Great Britain by
Midway Clark Printing, Wiltshire

Dedication
In memory of Frank Knowles – Reddish born and bred.

The cast of *Jack and the Beanstalk*, performed by members of St Elisabeth's church in the 1920s. They posed for the photograph in the backyard of Houldsworth school on St Elisabeth's Way. Behind them are the cloakrooms of the school. From the late 1890s the Sunday school staged these pantomimes in the school hall as the Amateur Pantomime Company.

Contents

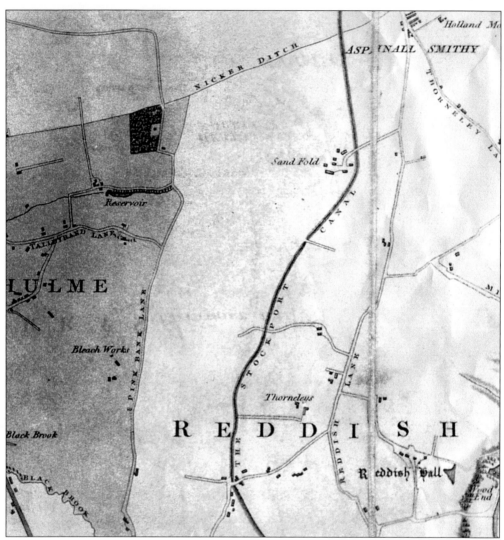

Johnson's map of Reddish of 1820 shows little development, with Sandfold an isolated hamlet in the north. Reddish developed as a linear town with the houses hugging the main roads. Pink Bank Lane forms the boundary with Levenshulme and Thorneley (or Thornley) Lane is Denton's border and Aspinall (or Aspinal) Smithy Gorton's. Nicker (or Nico) Ditch crosses the north end of the town. Mill Lane and Reddish Hall mark the edge of Reddish Vale, where Wood End was the print works' site.

Introduction

The town of Reddish, straddles the main roads between Gorton and Stockport, stretching from north to south on a long, narrow shelf of a hill, sloping down to the River Tame. Previously part of South Lancashire, in the parish of Manchester, Reddish became an Urban District Council in 1894. Lying two and a half miles north of Stockport centre, it passed under its control in 1901. To the north lie Gorton and Nico Ditch. On the east the Tame and Denton Brook form the boundary between Lancashire and Cheshire, Tameside and Stockport and the towns of Reddish, Denton, Brinnington and Bredbury. On the west Pink Bank Lane and Black Brook divide Reddish from Levenshulme and Heaton Chapel. To the south lie the River Mersey, Lancashire Hill and Portswood at Stockport. Variously spelled over the years Radich, Reddishe, Redyche and Redditch, the name means 'a ditch where reeds grow', possibly referring to Nico Ditch or one of the other brooks. The population grew from only 302 in 1774 with 54 houses, to 860 by 1831, 8,668 in 1901 and 14,252 by 1911.

From at least 1212, the lords of the manor were the de Reddish family, who lived at Reddish Hall on the edge of Reddish Vale, with the Hulme family at Hulme (later Broadstone) Hall. For years the countryside of Reddish was inhabited by hamlets of farmers, gradually enclosing the open land and relying on pastoral rather than arable farming, particularly cattle and dairy products.

By the early nineteenth century, there were three clusters of population. In North Reddish *Sandfold* formed an isolated hamlet. In the centre there was Great Reddish Green (the only surviving common land) around Barlow Fold, the Priory and the later Houldsworth estate and Little Reddish Green near Black Brook on Hulme (later Broadstone) Hall Road. The third area was in South Reddish, with Whitehill House as its nucleus. Hatting, hand- loom weaving and bleaching supplemented people's incomes from farming. Down in the vale a corn mill operated where Denton Brook meets the Tame.

The tithe map of 1844 shows 90 acres of arable land and 1,320 acres of meadow and pasture with 44 acres of buildings and streets. The main roads were along Gorton Lane (later Road) to Gorton, Reddish Road and Hulme Hall Lane to Stockport, Windmill Lane to Denton and along Mill lane or Reddish Vale Road across the vale. Mill Lane was a saltway, a packhorse route across the valley.

By the mid-nineteenth century the Stockport branch of the Manchester and Ashton canal (opened in 1797) and the railway routes across the vale, passing through Reddish North and Reddish South stations, brought industry and growth. From 1875 the Tame railway viaduct dominated the vale. Cotton mills began to spring up by the sides of the canal and a print works had opened in the 1750s down in the valley by the riverside.

Land ownership passed from the gentry, such as the Earl of Wilton, to the new cotton barons. Robert Hyde Greg and his family, who built the Victoria and Albert Mills, came to own most of South Reddish, plus parts of the centre and north. Sir William Houldsworth created his model industrial community, based on Houldsworth Mills, in central Reddish.

These new employers also considered the well-being of their workers, providing housing, social and welfare facilities, churches and schools and institutes. The Gregs built housing at Birkdale Road, Victoria Terrace and Greg Street, whereas Houldsworth planned a community near his mill. He also provided park and sports areas, the Houldsworth Institute and St Elisabeth's church, school and rectory, employing the architects, Waterhouse and Stott, to create this community. The Gregs helped to fund the building of St Mary's church and school and supported the Mechanics' Institute.

Various ironworks were opened in the town, including Furnival's in North Reddish with Furnival Street for the workers. There was also Jackson's brick works off Harcourt Street in

North Reddish. Terraces of red brick, well-built houses sprang up along and branching off the main roads.

This thriving working class, industrial community gave way to mansions of the well-to-do at the south end of the town, lining Reddish Road and the valley edges. Both Manchester and Stockport eyed this prosperous township and in 1901 Stockport took it under its control. By 1908 public buildings followed, the library, fire station and baths. The main roads were made-up, street lighting installed and the sewage system improved. In return Reddish surrendered some of her farmland for council housing but nothing high-rise, all semi's or maisonettes, such as 'Poets' Corner' off Longford Road West.

More recently, housing associations have created small complexes: Jubilee Court on Furnival's site, Russell Fox Court where Reddish Green Methodist church lay, plus Spey House and the Hayes.

The people of Reddish still form a community, retaining their rows of terraced housing and their individual, local shops, with no large supermarkets. In the early 1990s the residents successfully fought off a plan to sell off and develop part of Reddish Vale, which is now a country park, with the old print work's reservoirs and River Tame as centrepiece. There are two golf courses, Houldsworth and Reddish Vale, which both utilised family mansions as their clubhouses. Reddish Carnival was an outward symbol of the community spirit which has also fostered drama groups, football and cricket clubs, Rose queens and organisations for young people.

These photographs have been collected and assembled mainly from family albums and church archives. Many local people have helped to create this book, including Olive Lee who generously allowed me to use her paintings and photographs, and the Rector of St Elisabeth's, who permitted use of the church's collection of watercolours and drawings of Reddish from the 1880s. Former Rose and carnival queens, Whit walkers and producers of plays and processions have all contributed their photographs. The scenes on these photographs are often people centred, showing views along the streets and down in the vale, linking places with the people, associated with them. This collection of over 200 photographs includes church and school scenes, people in times of war and at leisure, as well as at home, work and out shopping.

Jill Cronin
January 2000

Acknowledgements

I should like to thank the following organisations and individuals for giving permission for their photographs to be included in this book. I have tried to locate everyone and apologise if anyone has been omitted.

Allan Arrowsmith, Jack and Edna Bedford, Joyce and Ron Brindley, Members of Christ Church, Mr R.R. Clark, Denton Local History Society, Marjorie Grantham, The Stan Horritt collection, Gordon Foy and Houldsworth Golf Club, Fay Kewley, Norah and Frank Knowles, Olive Lee, Jean Marlor, North Reddish Working Men's Club, The Quarry Bank Mill Trust Ltd, Andy Hart and Reddish Vale Golf Club, Frank Rhodes, The Rector and PCC of St Elisabeth's church, Marion and Harold Walton, Alan Ward, Ann Williams, Mr R.J.S. Wiseman, Mildred Wray.

One
Street Scenes

The junction of Mill and Windmill Lanes with Longford Road (left), c. 1910. The view is from Mill Lane, which continues right, down to Reddish Vale, past Mill Lane End Farm and Windmill Lane runs into the distance to meet Thornley Lane South, where it then makes its strange turns, to the right and then left. That point, marking the boundary between Reddish and Denton, is known as Blue Stone or Merestone. This large piece of granite was moved to Thornley Park but Bluestone Terrace and Road were named after it.

Tram car No. 32 of Manchester Corporation Tramway Co. operating on Reddish Lane, Gorton, near its terminus, by Athol Street in the 1940s. Laburnum Road, meeting Reddish Lane, forms Reddish's boundary with both Gorton and Denton. On the right is the old Aspinal church with its day and Sunday school beyond (see pp 59-60). The congregation came from Gorton, Reddish and Denton. Walling and plants, paid for by Manchester Corporation, replaced the wooden palings and privets when the road was widened.

Tram car No. 50 on Gorton Road (earlier Gorton Lane) by the Bull's Head public house, 1951. Stockport Corporation operated trams from Mersey Square and from Hazel Grove to Reddish from 1902, first to Greg Street, then to Vale Road and finally to connect with Manchester Corporation trams at Gorton's border. At the Bull's Head the trams would reverse and the trolley arm would be swung round.

Gorton Road just below Reddish North station, c. 1910. This busy scene contains plenty of people but few vehicles. Only the Stockport-bound tram, a hand cart and some other carts are visible. On the left, level with the tram, is the Railway Hotel with a large lantern outside. By the hotel is a row of shops called Market Place, built in 1878. Opposite lies the railway approach road.

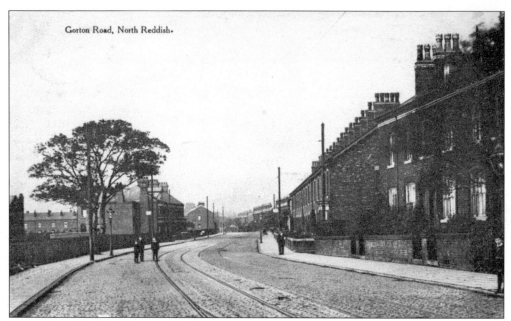

Gorton Road, North Reddish.

Gorton Road looking north towards Gorton, 1906. This view was taken from near Furnival's Ironworks, off to the left, where now new housing called Jubilee Court stands. There were also houses, dated 1886, for the workers along Furnival Street. Off to the right Ashbrook Lane led to Ashbrook's Farm, which today is a housing estate (see p. 30). Reddish North station lies north further up Gorton Road.

Gorton Road near Houldsworth Square, looking north towards Gorton, in the 1940s. Reddish police station is visible just beyond the tram, with the façade of St Joseph's Roman Catholic church opposite the station. On the right is the Gas Board showroom, which became the Houldsworth centre. Reddish has no town hall and this centre took on that role: rent and council tax could be paid and advice sought.

Gorton Road near Houldsworth Square in the late 1940s. On the right is the police station, which has now been converted to flats, with St Joseph's church opposite. On the right is Timothy White's and Taylor's chemist's shop with a fine clock outside. It later become Timothy White's and then Boot's. In the distance a bus is visible; buses were now beginning to replace the trams.

Gorton Road at its junction with Houldsworth Square in the late 1950s. On the right are the gas showrooms, next to Abram's florist and fruit shop, followed by Reddish post office and then the Maypole dairy. There was another Maypole at the north end of the town, in the row of shops opposite the Bull's Head public house. On the left is a row of shops called Reddish View 1842, where Birch's chemist's shop is.

Houldsworth Square, *c*. 1920. On the left is the Houldsworth clock and a drinking fountain, unveiled shortly after the First World War in memory of Sir William Houldsworth and erected by his grateful work force and the people of Reddish (see p. 38). On the left is a sign for Michelson's dining and tea rooms, where later was Birch's chemist's shop. Opposite, across Gorton Road, lies a row containing Palmer's sanitary engineers and Cooper's, bootmakers and repairers.

Houldsworth Square, viewed from Broadstone Road in the 1950s, with Leamington Road leading off to the left, from where a bus is emerging. Gorton Road is in the distant right, with Birch's chemist's shop on the left and the Maypole dairy is just out of view on the right. At the front left is Bridge's toy shop.

Houldsworth Square as it used to be. In the 1980s the clock was moved from its central position to the side of the square as part of traffic improvements. At the original unveiling of this memorial to William Houldsworth, a local alderman reputedly pronounced that, 'as Sir William, the clock should tell the same story on every face'. Sir William's likeness is on the plinth and there is a drinking fountain and trough. Broadstone Road runs on the left and the mill can be seen in the distance.

A cobbled Broadstone Road in the early 1900s. The road runs off Houldsworth Square and over the canal at Broadstone Bridge (visible in the distance) and so towards Heaton Chapel. Until Reddish became part of Stockport in 1901 most of the main roads were unlit and unsurfaced dirt tracks.

Reddish Road, Reddish.

Reddish Road in the early 1900s. On the left is the turning for Reddish Vale Road which, at this time, would have run past Reddish Hall Farm on its way down into the vale: now it runs over the site of the hall's moat, where the cinder road joined it. Beyond the large house on the left lay Yew Tree Farm. On the right is the turning for Greg Street, with Prescott's Almshouses on its far corner.

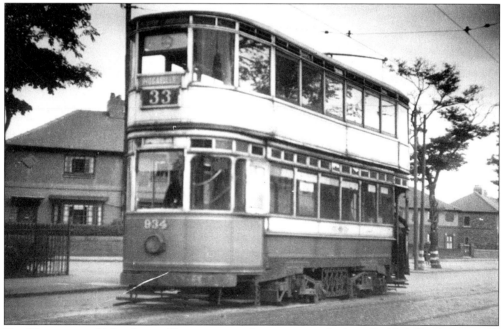

No. 33 tram car of Manchester Corporation makes it way north along Reddish Road, just south of the turning for Reddish Vale Road, heading towards the town centre and Manchester Piccadilly, in 1947. In 1879 Reddish Road became the first road to be lit in Reddish, from Reddish South station to the Stockport boundary.

Reddish Road in winter in the early 1900s. This former turnpike road was a winding country lane leading to Stockport, known as Sandy Lane between Reddish Green and Woodville. Rebuilt by Robert Greg to make it a straighter and a more efficient route to Stockport, it is often referred to as the New Road. The rather substantial gate posts visible in this picture show that the road at this time was becoming lined with the larger houses of the more affluent townspeople.

Reddish Road in the early 1900s. Many of these large houses set in their own grounds have now gone. A few survive, such as The Woodlands and The Grange, but gone are Woodville, Bella Vista, Willow Grove House and The Mount. The Carousel public house stands on the site of The Mount in an area once called Reddish Mount.

18

Two
Reddish Vale and Farming

Vale Road, Reddish.

This is Reddish Vale Road leading down past Reddish Vale Farm into the vale of the River Tame, depicted in a watercolour painting, *c*. 1880. The newly built railway viaduct of 1875 dominates this vale which was also renowned for its rare plants, fossils and crustaceans. Flowers such as the Purple Primrose, Hounds Tongue and Bluebell grew here. Blackberries flourished and a Blackberry Lane winds down to the vale from Brinnington.

Reddish Vale Road, looking down into the vale, c. 1912. The road still narrows to a country track past Reddish Vale Farm. There were other routes into the vale, including along Thornley Lane 'the road to the country' and Mill Lane, past Mill Lane End Farm. Roads led into the vale from all the neighbouring towns and footpaths criss-crossed it, including one over the railway by Red Bridge.

Reddish Vale Road running east down between cottages and Vale Farm in the 1890s. The cottages were originally built for the workers at the print works (see pp. 80/1). The farm was worked by the Watson family at the turn of the century (see p. 28). The horses from the print works were stabled here. This scene looks very similar today except that the stone gateposts have gone.

A row of cottages called Riverview, *c.* 1950. They were demolished in 1961, as were most other pockets of housing like this in the vale where once lived the railway viaduct navvies and farm and print workers. Riverview lay on the banks of the Tame on a cindered road near Sunnyside and Tame Houses (see p. 46). The fourteen houses in Riverview housed printworkers and had no electricity in the early 1900s.

The caption to this watercolour painting reads, 'The River Tame, just below Arderne Hall, looking west and downstream. Below Stockport this river is called the Mersey, Sept. 1 1879.' The river emerges at Haughton Dale from a sandstone gorge and meanders through the vale, creating water meadows which were a haven for wild plants in the sandy, clay soil. The local handloom weavers were said to have been good amateur botanists, scouring the vale for these plants.

The River Tame with Arden Hall on the distant hillside from a watercolour painting dated March 1879. Arden Hall lies on the Bredbury side of the vale but is part of the landscape of Reddish Vale (see p. 47). The river forms the boundary between Lancashire and Cheshire, Tameside and Stockport Metropolitan Boroughs and also between the towns of Denton, Reddish, Bredbury and Brinnington.

The River Tame flowing through the vale in the early 1900s. The scene on the right represents a rare example of arable farming in the area. The natural heavy clay forced farmers to convert to pastoral farming, after failed attempts to grow crops. Signs of the early ridge and furrow method of cultivation can still be seen in places. On the hillside is the row of houses that lines the way to Arden Hall.

Picnicking in Reddish Vale, c. 1913. Day trippers would travel from Gorton, Stockport, Levenshulme and other neighbouring towns to spend their weekends and bank holidays in the 'countryside' of Denton and Reddish. The area near Denton was called Bluebell Woods. Today the linear country park provides picnic areas, lakes for anglers and wildlife next to the former print work reservoirs, with meadows and woodland for walking, cycling, running and horse riding and Reddish Vale Golf Course (see p. 122).

Strines, Reddish Vale.

Strines Cottages in the vale in the early 1900s. These lay on the Brinnington side of the Tame above the weir, which together with large mill dams and a 700 yard mill race (constructed in the 1860s) provided a head of water for the print works. The three cottages, once a farm, are sometimes confused with the group of nine print workers' cottages by the railway viaduct (see pp 26-27, 47). Both sets of cottages have been demolished, Strines in 1939 and the nine cottages in around 1914.

A weir on the River Tame in the vale in the early 1900s with Strines Cottages in the background. Originally the weir and a millpond serviced a manorial corn mill, which straddled the water where the reservoirs for the print works later lay. Called Reddish Mill, it stood where the river met Denton Brook and between 1830 and 1840 became a school called The Ark but the building was demolished in about 1860 to make way for the reservoirs.

The River Tame in the vale in the early 1900s. In the distance is a works chimney. The river often became polluted from the mills, print works and sewage works and as it flowed on to become the Mersey it carried pollution to Stockport, causing complaints from that area. In the 1650s the river near the corn mill was known as Redich or Reddish Water. Today the M60 strides through the vale at its eastern end by Arden Hall.

The River Tame in the vale, 1905. On the right are Strines Cottages. In 1988 a mass protest rally of about 3,000 local people was effective in saving the vale from housing development on seventy of its acres. Accompanied by Gorton Silver Band the protesters marched down Mill Lane to gather at the Visitors' Centre. Finally in 1995 the 161 acres of the vale became Stockport's second country park, forming a linear park along the River Tame.

A skier on a temporary ski jump built in Reddish Vale in March 1960. Two Norwegian students at Manchester University had the idea of creating a ski jump platform on the Brinnington side of the vale. Twenty tons of snow, mixed with chemicals and ice to keep it frozen, were brought from Scotland. Volunteers helped to spread the snow for the two day event. The platform and ski ramp allowed 100 feet high jumps.

Competitors making the hard climb up to the ski platform. A crowd of over 15,000 people paid 2s 6d each to view the event. The money raised went to the World Refugee Year fund. In 1990 an attempt to set up an artificial ski slope on Woodhall fields was defeated by a 7,000 name petition. This one-off event had been welcomed but a permanent invasion of the vale was not.

The sixteen-arch Tame railway viaduct as it looked in the early 1900s. It belonged to the Sheffield and Midland Railways Committee and was built in 1875 to carry the line over the river. Lying north east of Reddish Vale print works, it crossed over the east end of its reservoirs. This row of cottages was called 'Nine Houses' and was home to local print workers (see p. 47). Nearby was Nine Houses Wood.

A train passing over the Tame viaduct in the early 1900s. This tall, brick built viaduct carried trains from Reddish North station south-east to Marple and New Mills. At the end of it was Reddish Junction where a branch line went south to Brinnington, Portwood and Tiviot Dale. This was eventually closed and taken up. From 1853, north of the viaduct, another line crossed it, joining the mineral railway from Denton Colliery to the depot at Reddish South. It is said that a local witch put a curse on the viaduct when it was built.

The 'royal train' of the London & North Western Railway passes over the Tame viaduct in 1905, heading for Manchester. It is possible that King Edward VII and Queen Alexandra were on board.

The farmhouse of Reddish Vale Farm, *c.* 1900. Vale Road passes between a row of cottages and this, nowadays whitewashed, house with its stables and yard (see p. 20). Print workers lived here and the horses from the works were stabled at the farm which was built in around 1887. George Watson farmed here in the early 1900s and Frank Stockton's family for over sixty years from 1931. In the early 1990s public saved prevented the now council-owned farm from development.

A caption on this watercolour painting reads, 'The only remaining portion of the old "Parian(?) gate". The rest has been altered and forms "Pink Bank Lane" extending from Rivett's Farm to Wingate House, Nov. 1880.' The area referred to is the western border of Reddish: Pink Bank Lane, together with Blackbrook, formed the town's boundary with Levenshulme and with the Heatons. Never made-up but once probably cobbled, this track is referred to in the records as 'a paved lane' and was the packhorse route from Stockport to Gorton. Wingate House later became the club house of Houldsworth Golf Club (see p.123).

Thompson's Farm from a watercolour dated 1883. This dairy farm at Reddish Green by the canal was farmed at that time by John and Emma Thompson. Their son James was the first child to be baptised in the assembly room of the Houldsworth Institute. Mr Hunt farmed there later and finally Mr Duncuft sold it, together with Jepson's (or Jephson's) Farm, to William Houldsworth, making sixty four acres for his mill complex.

Canal Bridge Farm, 1999. This white washed farmhouse with an attached barn lies just tucked in by Broadstone canal bridge, opposite Broadstone Mill. Since the 1960s this has been run by the Maben family as a dairy farm. In the 1840s, 1,320 acres of Reddish were pasture and meadow and 90 were arable. Cattle and milk production were very important and Reddish had numerous farms, nearly all now replaced by housing.

Ashbrook Farmhouse, on Ashbrook Lane, just prior to demolition in 1988. The farm lay between the railway and Criterion Street. John Ashbrook farmed there in the early years of the twentieth century until his death in 1908. The Ashbrook family is recorded in Reddish in the 1700s.

The rear of Ashbrook Farmhouse in 1988. A housing estate now covers this farm land and the only reminder of it lies in the name of Ashbrook Farm Close.

Three
People and Places

This watercolour shows, 'Sandfold from the canal, Sept. 12 1879.' The Stockport branch of the Manchester and Ashton Canal opened in 1797 and ran from Clayton, north to south along west Reddish, terminating at Lancashire Hill basin in Stockport. The canal provided transport and water for the mills' reservoirs. Disused by the 1930s, it was closed in 1962 and filled in. 'Sandfold' in North Reddish was the name used for a group of houses here from at least the 1600s.

Housing in Sandfold in 1997. This hamlet of thatched farmhouses and farm workers' cottages dates back to the 1600s. Four rows of white washed cottages stand in a fold at the end of the lane by the now filled-in canal, near to the border with Gorton and Nico Ditch. The lane was once also called Sandfold but was renamed Station Road, although a Sandfold name plaque still exists near Gorton Road.

Housing in Sandfold in 1997. In 1904 there was no other housing between Sandfold and the Bull's Head public house on Gorton Road. There was an area of water near here called variously 'Ashton Pits' or 'Hatters' Kettle'. The fold became less isolated when the railway brought industry and workers to the area. Two of the fields were known as 'Blue Caps' because of the blue bonnets of the Highlanders of Prince Charles, who were said to have encamped there in 1745, on their way to Derby.

Housing in Sandfold, 1997. There are records of burials at Gorton chapel in the 1600s and 1700s of the Oldham and Pickforth families of Sandfold or Sandhole. In the 1800s Mr Wood occupied the farm and the Bromleys, yeomen, lived in the fold, one of whom was treasurer of Gorton Sunday school. By 1904 the cottages were inhabited by ironworkers and labourers. Over the years there was a bleach works and fustian cutter's and hat works in this area.

Reddish North station in the 1980s. In 1875 a passenger service began from Ashbury's East near Belle Vue for Reddish Junction and on to Romiley. Originally called Reddish station, it was operated by the Manchester, Sheffield & Lincolnshire railway company, which became the Sheffield & Midland Joint and eventually the Great Central Railway. This station still has a fine Victorian, single-storey building on its south platform with a three bay iron and glass verandah.

John Aspinall near his home on Harcourt Street in 1939. Although the houses were built in around 1910, the street remained unmade until the early 1940s. There was one row of houses opposite Jackson's brickworks with its chimney and kilns. The open fields were known as Daisy or Brick Yard Fields with allotments, plus a duck pond. The view stretched as far as Werneth Low. Nearby was Summerfield House with an ornamental lake, a walled orchard and gardens.

Fanny (Fay) Aspinall on her wedding day in Harcourt Street, August 1939. Fay, who lived in Harcourt Street, married Harold Kewley, whose family were coal merchants in Reddish. For her wedding Fay wore a 'dusty pink' dress and hat, a fox fur and carried cream roses. Her dress had gold beads on the shoulder and down to her elbow. Fay was carnival queen in 1928 and Harold played football and the violin (see pp 93-95, 124-5, 128).

Stonework decoration on Reddish Library in Gorton Road, 1998. Stockport took control over Reddish in 1901 and one of the gains was this library in 1908, together with swimming baths and a fire station, which lie between Spencer and Melbourne Streets. They were built in fine Aston Hall brick with terrazzo flooring. By 1949 the library had lending and children's libraries and both general and ladies' reading rooms.

Reddish fire station and swimming baths, 1999. Once adorned by a flag pole and iron railings, both now gone, the fire station also included stable accommodation for the horses which drew the fire engine and rooms above the engine house for the firemen. A yard at the back enabled the fire engine to turn round. Today the fire station is used as a community centre. The baths included washing and bathing facilities as well as a swimming pool.

The towns' mortuary at the rear of the library, 1999. Here from 1908 the police would bring bodies on a small, narrow handcart covered by a black hood. This small building contained a marble slab and the firemen got paid extra for sewing the bodies into their shrouds. In the 1980s this mortuary was closed down and facilities transferred to Stockport.

Priory Mount at the end of Priory Lane is marked with a plaque dated 1891. In the 1920s Charles Merchant, the manager of Houldsworth Mills, lived here. It lay opposite the land of Mr Shawcross, partner at the nearby hat works, who built Summerfield which, from 1908, has been the Conservative Club. Later Mr Lowe, the owner of Lowe's chemical works, owned and enlarged Summerfield, whose grounds originally stretched from Harcourt Street across Gorton Lane to here.

The hat works of Barlow & Shawcross off Gorton Road with Priory Lane on the right, 1777. In the grounds stood the Priory, home to one of the owners, Samuel Barlow and also cottages for his workers. His colleague, Mr Shawcross lived in nearby Summerfield House. When the canal opened nearby, they erected a footbridge over it to link with the footpath across the field to their works. In around 1850 Mr Hamer, a Manchester brewer, bought the works and Priory Lane became Hamer's Lane. In around 1890 the works were demolished, but the house survived (see below).

Reddish police station on Gorton Road near Houldsworth Square in the 1990s. Above the doorway are the arms of the County palatine of Lancaster, which Reddish was part of until Stockport took control in 1901. There were plans to turn the station into a youth club but they were abandoned. A modern, single storey police station was built in 1982 further along Gorton Road, nearer to Gorton. The old station has now been renovated and converted into flats.

Sir William Henry Houldsworth MP, 1834-1917, regarded as the maker of modern Reddish. Born in Ardwick, he was Conservative MP for Manchester 1883-1905 and a baronet from 1887. He died in Scotland aged 82. Believing that God had allotted each his station in life, he provided sickness benefit and saving schemes for his workers. He was a prime mover in the building of Manchester's Houldsworth Hall and Church House (headquarters of the Manchester Diocese). A clock was erected in his memory in Houldsworth Square (see p. 16).

Houldsworth conservation area, 1997. Sir William Houldsworth bought farmland here in 1864 on which to build his cotton mills, St Elisabeth's church (centre), rectory and school, park and sports club, working men's club (top right) and planned housing for his workers. He employed the architect Alfred Waterhouse to design the church, rectory and school and Abraham Henthorn Stott to design the Houldsworth Institute and the mills. Together they created a model industrial community which is now a conservation area.

Alfred Waterhouse, architect, ARA, FRIBA, was born in 1830 and trained in Manchester. He was an exponent of Victorian Gothic or Romanesque style. Among his designs are Manchester's Assize Courts, Town Hall and Owen's College now Manchester University, Salford Jail and numerous mansions, schools, churches and other public buildings, including those at Reddish.

Housing on Houldsworth Street, opposite Houldsworth Mills, 1997. These houses are more substantial than the rest in this complex, having bay windows and front gardens. They were probably built for the foremen and overlookers and were thus nicknamed 'Nob Row'. In 1904 they were inhabited by cotton spinners, carders and mechanics, probably all employed at the mills opposite.

Houldsworth Park, c. 1910. This park, recreation grounds and sports club were opened in July 1910, as a gift to Stockport from Sir William Houldsworth. Originally there were iron railings. In the first section was the school football ground, next swings and a see-saw, then a shelter, toilets and the gardens themselves.

Houldsworth Park in the late 1940s. North Reddish Park was opened on the site of Fir Tree Farm on Gorton Road in around 1948: 'A new park has recently been laid out, which combines facilities for recreation in a horticultural setting to a very pleasant degree.' There were also South Reddish Park and playing fields set out in north and south Reddish in 1949 and at St Joseph's on the site of twelve shops near Prenton View and Schofield Street.

Housing on Liverpool Street, part of the original Houldsworth complex, 1999. Some streets have been demolished, spoiling the original planned area, to the east of which were more modest houses with four rooms, yards and privvies. Other mill owners provided housing for their workers too: Robert Greg built Greg Street and Birkdale Road in the mid-nineteenth century and Victoria Terrace above Victoria Mill on Broadstone Hall Road South in 1845.

St Elisabeth's church and the Houldsworth Institute on Leamington Road, 1906. Consecrated in 1883 (see pp 54-56), it was design by Alfred Waterhouse. The institute, opened in 1874, with its large bow window and ornamental roof, with dormers and gables, is a distinctive building. By 1878 it contained reading, meeting and billiard rooms, plus a library, lecture hall and bowling green. Sir William believed in fostering the moral well being of his workers, encouraging their thrift and industry. No politics, gambling or swearing were allowed.

Broadstone canal bridge over the Stockport branch of the Manchester and Ashton Canal, looking south, c. 1905. These cottages lay behind Houldsworth Mill. When Broadstone Road was widened in 1910 they were demolished. Behind them, across the road, Broadstone Mill is visible, then in the process of being built. The warm waters near the mills were often home to goldfish and exotic plants, brought in with the cotton imports, and attracting children for swimming.

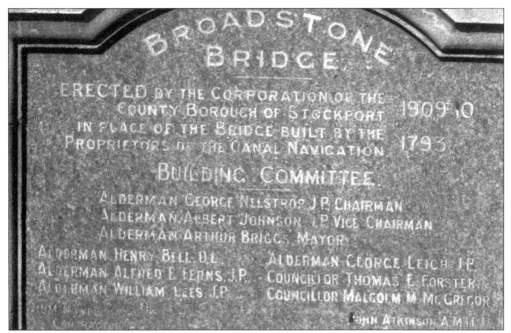

The stone on Broadstone canal bridge, commemorating its reopening after rebuilding, as part of the widening of Broadstone Road, 1910. The original bridge had been constructed in 1793, when the canal project was started. The mayor, Ald. Arthur Briggs, declared it open on 16 July 1910.

A row of cottages on the Broadstone Mill side of Broadstone canal bridge, 1999. This terraced row survives, tucked in by the bridge. The large cottage in the middle, a conversion from two cottages, is known as Ivy or Cosy Cottage. Up until around 1890 it housed the Yew Tree Inn, which brewed its own beer. In 1852 James Selby was the landlord with a twenty one year agreement to pay £8 rent annually. The back gates led onto the towpath of the canal and behind there was also a planking shop for hatting.

An advertisement for housing on Broadstone Hall Road in the 1940s. The road was originally called Bowlas or Bowlais Lane as well as, at other times, Aston or Hulme Hall Road. The Bowlas were a farming and mill owning family and Hulme Hall was the earlier name of Broadstone Hall. The road leads from Stockport through Reddish to Ashton. Housing on that road was intermixed with mills such as the Spur, the Victoria and the Hammond House Works.

Broadstone or Hulme Hall in the 1880s. The hall, originally the home of the Hulme family who held land in Reddish from the thirteenth century, was rebuilt in 1637 and again in the mid 1800s. The two names co-existed until Broadstone became its final name. The estate covered 225 acres in 1844. It became a farm but was demolished in 1945, becoming the site of Broadstone Hall primary school. William Hulme founded Hulme Grammar school and set up scholarships for the poor at Oxford in 1691.

The front view of Reddish Hall, off Reddish Vale Road, looking east over the River Tame. This black and white plaster and half-timbered house, with three overhanging gables at the front, stood on a stone plinth. Inside there was a great hall, a domestic chapel and a 'priest's chamber' over the gateway. The estate covered 535 acres in 1844. Originally on a quadrangular, moated site, the hall was demolished in around 1780, when a farm of that name was built nearby. Reddish Vale School now occupies this site.

Tame House in Reddish Vale near the print works. At one time home of the manager of the print works, it was later used as offices by the Calico Printers' Association. Beyond it lay Riverview, a row of cottages by the river. Nearby was Sunnyside, the home in the 1890s of Robert Hammond, who ran the works as Bradshaw, Hammond & Co. It later became a social club for the calico printers.

THE LATE MISS LYDIA BECKER.
(From a Photograph by Warwick Brookes.)

Miss Lydia Becker, a campaigner for women's rights in the Suffragette movement, was born in 1827. Her brother Ernest Hanniball Becker ran Reddish Vale print works in the 1840s under the name of Becker Bros & Co. Lydia lived with him in the vale near the works for a while. She was a keen amateur botanist. She spent her life, through writing and lecturing, campaigning for votes for women. She was secretary of the National Society for Women's Suffrage from 1867 and a member of the Manchester School Board in the 1870s.

Part of the row of cottages known as Nine Houses tucked in by the railway viaduct in Reddish Vale, 1879. They stood very near the site of the corn mill, overlooking the reservoirs of the print works. Built in around 1820, they were home to the workers who built the viaduct as well as to calico printworkers. Here visitors to the vale could purchase jugs of hot water or pots of tea. The cottages were demolished in around 1914.

Ardern (also Arden, Arderne and Harden) Hall in Reddish Vale on the banks of the River Tame in the early 1900s. Although this lies on the Bredbury or Cheshire side of the vale, the Arderne family played a large part in the history of both Denton and Reddish. Built probably in the sixteenth century, the hall was moated and in a fine defensive position on Castle Hill. The Arderne coat of arms was carved on the front wall but the site belonged originally to the de Bredburys.

Part of Prescott's Almshouses on Reddish Road at the corner of Greg Street, 1999. Erected in 1882 to a design by James Hunt, these six terraced houses were built with money left by W.W. Prescott, a drysalter to the hat trade. He left £5,000 for 'the infirm and old' living in the 'ancient townships of Denton, Bredbury and Reddish'. His trustees decided to build and maintain these houses for six poor women, who were paid 4s a week and who lived rent free.

Robert Hyde Greg, son of Samuel Greg of Quarry Bank Mill, Styal, 1795-1875. Along with William Houldsworth, Robert is regarded as one of the makers of modern Reddish as an industrial and residential district. The Gregs came to own most of the south and parts of central and north Reddish. Robert, with his brother John, built Victoria and Albert Mills with housing for their workers. He was committed to the idea of the Mechanics' Institutes and to the social welfare of his workers. An MP for Manchester from 1839-1841, he retired from the Reddish mills in 1858.

The Grange at the corner of Reddish Road and Redland Avenue, 1999. Reddish Road was lined with the houses and gardens of the well-to-do (see pp 17-18). Now a residential home, the Grange was once home to Joseph Marsland, a cotton mill owner in Heaton Chapel. The Marsland's groom, James Ford, lived in one of two thatched cottages in what is now Redland Avenue that were demolished for development in the 1920s. In 1904 Frank Reed, an engineer, lived at the Grange.

Southcliff, off Southcliffe Road and Reddish Road, 1999. This the only survivor out of a group of three large houses (also Broomfield and Woodville),that stood in its own grounds on the slopes of the vale and was famous locally for its gardens. In 1891 Frederick Scott, owner of the Atlas steel wire ropeworks near Greg Street on Reddish Road, lived there. It has been the club house of Reddish Vale Golf Club since 1912 (see p. 122).

Ann Williams with her dog outside Southcliff Cottages, within the grounds of Southcliff, 1980. By 1904 Sarah Scott still lived at Southcliff and this was the home of her coachman George Smith and her gardener William Smith. In around 1942 Ann William's uncle bought the left-hand cottage, which he greatly altered. Then her other uncle moved into the right-hand one, giving them both easier access to their war work at A.V. Roe & Co.

The rear view of Southcliff Cottages, 1999. On the right is the extended cottage of Ann William's uncle, into which Ann moved in 1976. The cottages had been used earlier to house the grooms and estate workers and then by the golf club for their professional player. Originally the cottages had two rooms with a kitchen/scullery downstairs and three bedrooms upstairs and an outside toilet. Lighting was by gas mantle and cooking was on a coal range.

Four
At Church

The curate of St Agnes' church , the Revd Werwath, with a confirmation class, in around 1961. St Agnes in North Reddish was the third Anglican church to be opened in the town. Starting life as a mission room in 1880, it continued as an iron-built church in 1882 on land rented from the Earl of Wilton, moving to its present site in 1908. Formed from part of St Elisabeth's parish, it draws its congregation from Denton, Reddish and South Manchester.

The fire, which destroyed the 'iron church', the mission church of St Agnes' which stood on land rented from the Earl of Wilton, on the corner of Midland Road and Ashford Street, opposite North Reddish working men's club, on the left (see p.120). The church was opened by the Revd Crofton's wife and first used as a Sunday school, when the new church, designed by L. & T. Mayer, was opened on Gorton Road in 1908. At the time of this photograph in the 1970s the building was occupied by a private firm.

The wedding of Joyce Allison and Ron Brindley at St Agnes' church, 1968. Ron was a member of the choir and so both the choir and the organist, Sam Blackburn (fifth from the left), attended the wedding. Behind the group is the original front door to the church and plain brick wall, which have twice since undergone alteration. On the right are houses in St Agnes' Street.

The lych gate and window of St Agnes' church in the 1980s. In 1968 a new porch and this window, forty feet high and modelled on the baptistry at Coventry Cathedral, replaced the original plain front. Each pane commemorated a church member. In 1992 a new porch replaced the window, as it was found to be unsafe and had to be demolished.

The wedding of Susan Walton and Howard Lawes at St Agnes' church, 1972. On the right is Susan Venning and on the left Kath Scott. The group is standing outside the stained glass window, which replaced the earlier plain wall and front door. The church had cost £6,000 to build but this wall had been left plain.

The altar of St Agnes' church. Behind lies the stained glass of the east window dedicated to the first rector, Spencer Gibb (1902-1928). Other windows are dedicated to the Mothers' Union's 21st anniversary (1929-1950), to Annie Beatrice Birchall, to church warden Thomas Hanson Smith and to St Oswald. The Lady chapel window recalls Addison Crofton, priest at St Elisabeth's, and his mother Anne Agnes of the Mission church. Sir William Houldsworth donated the organ which was dedicated in 1913.

The interior of St Elisabeth's church with its unique alabaster and marble, Venetian screen, topped with marble figures of the four Evangelists. The altar rests in an apse decorated with mosaics. The lofty nave with its ribbed, cradle roof rests on sandstone columns which were delivered to the site by elephants from Belle Vue Zoo. The stained glass windows have been called 'the triumph of Faith'. The Houldsworth chapel has a memorial to Sir William, who commissioned Waterhouse to design the adjacent rectory in 1875.

St Elisabeth's church with the Houldsworth Institute on the right in the 1880s. This first photograph of the church, showing the wall still unfinished and the road unpaved, was taken by Robert Marsden. The man in the photograph is Robert Bates whose memorial tablet is now in the church. The style is Victorian Gothic Revival, mixed with Byzantine and Norman features. Waterhouse's inspiration was the Basilica of St Mark's church in Venice. The parish was the second to be formed in Reddish from parts of St Mary's, Reddish, and St Thomas', Heaton Chapel. The church was started in a mission room in 1873 by the Revd Addison Crofton, appointed by Sir William to minister to his workforce.

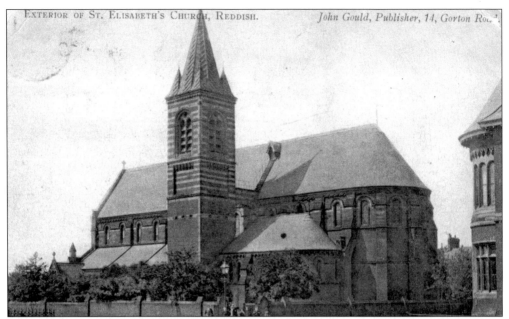

St Elisabeth's church on Leamington Road with, on the right, the Houldsworth Institute 1905. It was consecrated in 1883, named after Lady Houldsworth and paid for entirely by Sir William. On the roof is an external flight of stone steps forming a bridge linking the tower with its eight bells, to the church. The dressed stone came from Wrexham and the unusually thin, red bricks from Openshaw.

St Mary's mission church on Ann Street, built in 1860 and nicknamed 'the salt box'. The move to build a church came from Heaton Norris and so came the name Heaton Reddish for South Reddish. A room at Lancashire Hill became a schoolroom for poor children from Reddish and from Heaton Norris and the Revd Francis Parsons took services in a licensed room.

A watercolour of St Mary's church on Reddish Road, South Reddish by Olive Lee, from the 1980s. Consecrated in 1865, it was designed by Shellard and Brown and seated 400. This was the first Anglican church in the town. Robert Greg donated one acre of farmland and the foundation ceremony included a procession and a 'cold collation' provided by Belle Vue. This stone building is in the Perpendicular style and is without the tower that was originally intended and proved too costly. Its windows are decorated with small columns for mullions.

St Joseph's Roman Catholic church on Gorton Road in the early 1900s. Consecrated in 1882, this building was paid for largely by Joseph Higginson. The congregation increased rapidly in size in the late nineteenth century with the influx of Irish immigrants to work in the local cotton mills. The church included two classrooms and later a church hall and an adjoining presbytery on Gorton Road.

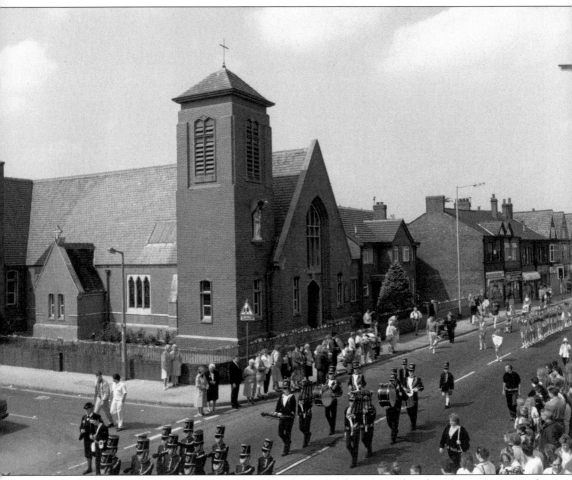

St Joseph's Roman Catholic church in the 1990s. In the 1960s the church was extensively rebuilt with an east extension. The altar was moved from east to west and this tower erected next to the new main entrance. The fifty feet high tower is of Accrington brick surmounted by a red neon cross. The school was also extended.

Laying of the foundation stone of Aspinal (or Aspinall) Wesleyan Methodist church on Reddish Lane, July 1909. The church actually lies in Gorton but was part of the Stockport circuit, drawing its congregation also from Denton and Reddish, as it borders all three towns. From around 1795 services were held at Brook Green Farm, until the first church was built in 1808. A growth in congregation entailed opening a larger chapel alongside it in 1877 (visible in the background) and this one followed in 1910.

Aspinal Centenary chapel on Reddish Lane, 1910. The former church of 1808 became the Day/Sunday school, until demolition in 1886 to build a new school. This church was called Centenary because it was built about 100 years after the first chapel of 1808. On a site given by Thomas Wild and the Misses Wild, it was designed by A.E. Lambert of Nottingham and cost £5,500. The title Aspinal is thought to be from a local family name.

The interior of Aspinal Smithy Centenary chapel, 1910. There was seating for 850 people. The semi-Gothic effect included a pulpit and choir of oak. This third church was demolished in 1972, as the size of the congregation dwindled and a smaller church was opened with a separate sanctuary and place for concerts and social activities.

The opening of the Centenary or third church building of Aspinal Smithy Methodist church, 1910. The minister was the Revd Hugh Saunders. The exterior was of Ruabon brick with stone facings and a square tower.

The first Wesleyan Methodists in Reddish began regular meetings in the loom room of No. 121 Broadstone Road (second from left), after meeting in various houses from around 1830. The first church was on Broadstone Road in 1860 and consisted of a large room with two vestries and a porch.

The interior of the second church of Reddish Green Methodists which was built in 1870. This church lay just past Rupert Street on Broadstone Road. Known as the 'school chapel', it cost £2,000 and could seat 550. In 1887 a Sunday school was added, which was used for a while by Houldsworth school, as they awaited their new building (see p.68).

The second church of Reddish Green Methodists, before 1904. The original layout contained this single room on the left with no transepts or separate chancel. On the left is Broadstone Road leading to Houldsworth Square. On the right is the Sunday school.

Reddish Green Methodist church, viewed from Broadstone Road in 1976. This, and the view below, were recorded before the congregation moved in 1978 to Christ church to join with the Congregationalists, known from 1973 as the United Reformed church. In 1904/5 Reddish Methodist church had been enlarged by adding two transepts and two vestries (right) and building a separate chancel.

The interior of Reddish Green Methodist church in 1976. The altar is viewed from the vestibule, from where it was moved in 1904 into this extended chancel with new choir stalls. The pulpit was also moved to this end and the front door was created where the organ had stood (see p.61).

The interior of Reddish Green Methodist church in 1976. Viewed from the chancel, this is the same view as on page 61 but the altar and organ have now been transferred to the opposite end, with a screen and porch replacing them. On one side was a choir and on the other the minister's vestries. Following demolition, a housing development, called Russell Fox Court, occupied the site. Fox was a local preacher and church trustee who became a local councillor and Mayor of Stockport.

The wedding of Alice Aspinall to James Brittain at Christ Church Congregational church in the 1940s. Second front left is Alice's bridesmaid, her sister Fay, wearing her own bridal outfit (see pp 34, 93-95). The best man on the left is James' brother and Alice's father, John, and her mother, are on the right at the back.

Five

At School

A class at North Reddish council school with their teachers in the 1920s. These pupils from the senior section of the school are seen here after being presented with a shield and a painting. The painting is of Dante meeting Beatrice by the River Arno in Florence.

The Houldsworth day school of St Elisabeth's church, seen here in 1985, opened in 1876 and was designed by Waterhouse. From 1871 the school was held in Reddish Green Methodist church, moving to the Institute in 1874 and then to this building, which had three main rooms with two classes attached to each room. The distinctive, high windows give elegance and light to a building, once described by inspectors as one of the finest school buildings in the north of England.

Children coming out of Houldsworth school at St Elisabeth's in the late 1960s or early 1970s. In 1871 there were 84 pupils, 316 by 1880 and 371 in 1888. In 1898 the school was enlarged again and housed 881 pupils.

The centenary celebrations of the Houldsworth school, 1976. Former pupils and staff enjoyed services in the church and on this evening gathered in the school. In 1953 the governors had decided to retain church control as an Aided school. In 1987 the building was remodelled.

St Agnes' church Sunday school on Beresford Crescent in around 1987. When the new church was opened in 1908 the mission church was used as a Sunday school, until this church hall became the Sunday school. In 1989 this was sold and the land was used for housing.

Reddish Green Methodists' Sunday school and church, viewed from Rupert Street in 1976. On the left is the church, which was enlarged in 1904 with the school on the right, to the rear, which had been added in 1887. The school was used briefly by the pupils of Houldsworth school, while awaiting completion of their own building. Both school and church were demolished in 1978.

A group of children outside North Reddish council school, *c.* 1916. The school stands at the corners of Longford, Denstone and Lewis Roads, all of which appear unmade in this picture. This council school supplemented the church schools as the local population grew. Although built in 1907, it did not open until 1916, because the buildings were used as a military hospital during the First World War. The school was opened with 460 juniors and 200 infants. A senior section was added later to cater for pupils up to fourteen years.

Standard 4 of North Reddish council school with their teacher Miss Sale, 1921. In the second row from the front, second left, is Frank Aspinall and third, Harold Kewley. The oldest school seems to have been the Ark (opened between 1830-40) at the corn mill in Reddish Vale, straddling Denton Brook and so called because water could be seen through the floor boards! It was demolished in around 1860 to make way for the extension of the reservoirs of Reddish Vale print works.

Class 11 of North Reddish council school in July 1924. Most churches had their own Sunday and day schools, including St Elisabeth's, St Mary's, St Joseph's and St Anne's. Other council primary schools were opened as the population grew, including Fir Tree, Broadstone Hall and Abingdon Road.

Class 12 of North Reddish council school in July 1924.

Class 10 of North Reddish council school in October 1928.

Class 12 of North Reddish council school in October 1928. On the left is the teacher Miss Fricker with her class of seven year olds. Holding the board is Marion Walton (née White).

Standard 5 Seniors of North Reddish council school in 1931. Miss Hamnett is in the centre and third from the left on the back row is Marion Walton (née White).

The juniors of class 11 of North Reddish council school, September 1929.

Standard Ex 7 Seniors of North Reddish council school in September 1935. This was an advanced class for those pupils about to leave. Miss Sayle is the teacher and fifth from right Marion Walton can be seen again. Mr Hiles was head of the senior department at that time, Mr Harrsion of the juniors and Miss Burnett of the infants. In 1944 seven classes (in six rooms) became North Reddish Secondary Modern school.

Class 10 of North Reddish council school in September 1935.

A football team at St Mary's school, 1958/9. Opened as the Albert British school on Greg Street opposite the working men's club in 1864, St Mary's was enlarged in 1898. Catering for 338 children, it was the first proper school in Reddish. Until St Mary's church was opened in 1865, services were held at the school, which also housed the Mechanics' Institute and a library for local people, this being the town's first public library. A new school was eventually built at the vale end of Broomfield Drive.

A class at Reddish Vale Secondary Modern school in the 1950s. The building looks almost new here as the school was only opened in 1952, on the site of the farm which had replaced Reddish Hall. The first head, Mr Griffiths, stayed from 1945 to 1965.

A class at Reddish Vale Secondary Modern school in 1954. In 1987 the school became a Comprehensive and then a Technical College in 1995. In the early 1990s there was a small farm at the school, which was visited by children from the local nurseries and infants' schools. This community school added a swimming pool and sports centre in 1994 and a theatre in 1998.

Six
Work and Shopping

Houldsworth Mill on Houldsworth Street near Leamington Road with Houldsworth recreation ground in the foreground, early 1900s. Originally farmland this area was acquired by Sir William Houldsworth in 1864 became the site of his cotton mills and industrial community. Opened in 1865, in spite of a cotton famine, it was one of the largest double mills to be built at that time. Designed by Abraham Stott of Oldham and lying at the side of the Ashton canal, this fine, red brick, Italianate style, mill is perfectly symmetrical.

Houldsworth Mill, looking straight up Rupert Street, with workers' houses built by Houldsworth, on the right. The five-storey central block, crowned by a clock tower, was erected in 1865. The clock has two faces and neede two men to wind it up. The tower was flanked by stairway towers. It really is a double mill with two eighteen bay spinning mills, joined by a central office block and warehouse, with an engine house behind and an unusually tall chimney built on an octagonal base.

The interior of Houldsworth Mill, 1997. The rows of cast iron pillars are closely set to give strength to support the weight of the mules used for spinning. The beams also are of cast iron and the arches are of brick. The blocks are wider than in earlier mills as the mules were greater in length in the 1860s. On the ground floor the cotton was prepared for the power spinning mules on the upper three floors, where at its peak the mill contained 140,000 spindles.

Decoration on a cast iron column supporting the roof in Houldsworth Mill, 1997. The transverse brick-vaulted ceiling is supported by cast-iron beams and these columns. Everything is of fireproof construction. In 1898 the firm amalgamated with the Fine Cotton Spinners & Doublers Association. By 1958 cotton production had ceased and the mill took on a multi-purpose function with a rear extension added onto the north wing in the 1960s. In 1997 Prince Charles visited the mill, now a Grade Two listed building, which is to became a business, residential and leisure complex.

The Reddish Spinning Company mills, lying north of Houldsworth Mill between Houldsworth Street and the canal with a mill dam. The oldest section, the Little Mill, was opened in 1870 with Houldsworth as chairman. The mill was a more developed structure than Houldsworth Mill, having up to 132,200 spindles and 400 employees. The New Mill, opened in 1877, was also a red brick, four-storey building but it had cast iron columns and a brick arch floor, whereas the Little Mill had wooden floors and beams. The smaller, later, two-storey Park View Mill has been demolished.

Vol. V. No. 13.   JANUARY, 1932.

"Fancy Yarns"

R. GREG & Co LTD
STOCKPORT

FOR OURSELVES
by
OURSELVES

The front cover of the house journal of R. Greg & Co. from the 1930s. This journal continued for forty years from 1921, stopping only during the Second World War. It kept the workers in touch, aired their views and passed on information, and is now avaluable record of mill life. The Gregs, concerned for the welfare of their employees, provided a doctor, optician and dentist at their mills and recreational facilities, including a gymnasium and playing fields. They owned most of south and parts of north and central Reddish.

An advertisement for R. Greg & Co. at Albert Mill, Greg Street, 1951. In 1845 Robert Hyde Greg (son of Samuel of Quarry Bank Mill) opened this mill named the 1845 Mill. Extensions and other mills followed on this canalside site in 1907 and in the 1920s. Spinning and doubling took place with 48,728 ring spindles and 31,128 doubling spindles by 1951. Fancy yarns were their speciality. In the 1970s the firm was still family run but in 1982 with new owners, the mills closed and housing development of the site followed. Its companion mill, Victoria, still stands.

An advertisement for the Spur Doubling Mill which lay south of Broadstone Hall Road South, between Greg Street and the canal, c. 1948. Opened in 1909, the firm specialised in the doubling of fine cotton yarns for the lace, hosiery and lisle trades. In the 1920s they took over the Moor Mill of the Bowlas family, producing 'heavy doubled' cotton yarn. By 1951 there were 23,000 spindles at Spur Mill, employing 400 people. In 1972 the firm closed down but the building remains.

Reddish Vale print works from an engraving of the 1770s. Opened in the 1750s as a calico bleach and dye works, this firm lay on the west bank of the Tame in the vale, using the river to power the machinery. By 1787 Messrs Thorpe & Paul ran the firm and lived nearby. By 1825 calico printers, John Fletcher & Radcliffe, were here. In the 1940s Becker Bros ran four printing machines with 118 block printing tables. Two small reservoirs were constructed to the northwest to hold the water, with a 700 yard long mill race from the former weir and mill pond of the earlier corn mill.

Reddish Vale print works by the River Tame probably in the 1930s. In 1862 Bradshaw, Hammond & Co. operated here as machine calico printers until the early 1900s. In 1899 they amalgamated with the Calico Printers' Association, having thirteen machines and around 330 employees. The whole process of singeing, bleaching, washing, printing, dyeing, ageing, stentering and finishing took place on one site. Exports went as far as India, Egypt, the Levant, Africa, the Balkans and America.

Employees setting off on an outing from the Reddish Vale print works, *c.* 1930. Behind them their charabanc awaits. The works site consisted of single- and two-storey buildings with an engine house and an octagonal brick chimney, plus reservoirs. Although calico printing ceased in around 1979, the site continued to be used as a small industrial estate until 1997. Today the reservoirs are fish ponds and the Reddish Vale Visitors' centre nearby promotes the delights of the vale.

An advertisement for J.T. Gibson & Sons Ltd, sheet metal workers, of 43, Lambeth Road, *c.* 1948. James Gibson established the firm in 1887 and eventually employed twenty people, supplying engineers and manufacturers.

The abandoned works site of Reddish Gas Engine Works, just north of Reddish South station in 1999. Established in 1886 by J. Andrew in Stockport, the firm employed 100 men in Reddish, opening there in 1887. Andrew developed the Stockport horizontal gas engine, an offshoot of the Bischop gas engine. In 1906 he amalgamated with Richard Hornsby & Sons Ltd of Grantham and then in 1918 with Ruston, Procter & Co of Lincoln, after which it became known as Ruston & Hornsby's Gas & Oil Engine Works.

Mr Joseph Bowers of 60, Park Street, Ashton-under-Lyne, after his fifty years service presentation of a gold medal and an easy chair by the firm of Ruston & Hornsby Ltd in 1930. In 1904 an iron foundry had been added to the works and there were offices fronting the main road near the station entrance. When the Reddish site was closed down the Stockport gas engines continued to be made and sold for some time afterwards.

An advertisement for the Storey Foundry Co. Ltd on Conway Street, South Reddish, *c.* 1948. Other engineering firms included Charles Rushton, boiler maker and heating engineer on Sandy Lane, South Reddish which was established around 1880. Furnival's iron works, lying between Gorton Road and the canal off Furnival Street, North Reddish, moved onto a fourteen acres site in 1880 to produce printing presses and gas engines. Furnival Street was built for their workers in 1886.

A panoramic view of Craven Brothers' Vauxhall Works which were located on both sides of Greg Street, in the early 1900s. They moved from the Vauxhall Works in Manchester to these larger premises, by the railway on this thirteen and a half acres site in 1900. The firm retained the Vauxhall name and produced cranes and machine tools for the railways and for engineering generally. By the 1920s the site covered over twenty two acres and employed 1,300 workers, growing later to twenty five acres and employing 1,400 workers.

The office block for Craven Brothers' Vauxhall Works on Greg Street, under construction in 1913. This two-storey building, fronting onto Greg Street, has a date-stone of 1914. The north side of the site had the foundry and offices and the south side the main works. The First World War was starting so they did not transfer fully into the new offices until 1920. The top floor contained the drawing room with 100 designers, draughtsmen and estimators.

A view of the iron foundry at Craven Brothers' Vauxhall Works. Castings of up to forty five tons weight were produced here with a small, separate foundry producing non-ferrous castings. All heavy moulding work was transferred to this Reddish site, where the foundry, crane and pattern shops were built first. Next came the smithy, pattern stores and machine tool departments. In 1939 the Victoria Works were built in Denton where another foundry supported the one here at Reddish.

A large casting being transported from the foundry at Craven Brothers' to the heavy machinery department. Railway sidings served all departments across this spacious yard. In 1931 Craven's sold off their crane business and concentrated on producing machine tools. In 1970 these works were closed following a take over by Staveley machine tools.

The printworks mill with its ornamental clock tower, on the west side of Greg Street, north of Victoria Mill, 1987. This was originally the print works of the *Manchester Guardian* and opened in 1899. In 1919 it became the printworks of the Co-operative Wholesale Society, as a branch of their Longsight offices, until that closed. The Co-op also had a jam and sweet making works at the end of Hurst Street.

The milk delivery cart belonging to Reddish Vale Farm, 1918. Gladys Watson, whose family farmed there in the early 1900s, is on the cart (see p 28).

The corner shop on Reddish Vale Road, opposite Reddish Vale Farm, *c.* 1913. By the door stands Mrs Bromley. The shop provided a welcome service for the farm and for the print workers and farm labourers, who lived in the adjoining houses. The shop no longer operates but the building exists as a private house.

Ashford's DIY Stores at the corner of Gorton and Midland Roads, 1995. This business was established in around 1945 and grew to become this large store near Reddish North station. This photograph shows the premises for sale when the firm closed down. The store is now demolished.

Mr Allison in the doorway of his ironmonger's shop at 606, Gorton Road, in the 1950s. The Allison family lived above the shop, which was run by Walter and then his son Arthur. They sold household electrical goods, hardware and tools, had a hand turned key cutting machine and dispensed paraffin. Opposite was the Bull's Head public house. On the right were Finn's cobbler's shop, then Margaret's sweet shop and Wardle's cycle and toy shop. On the left was a grocer's shop.

Allison's ironmonger's shop on Gorton Road in the 1950s. The array of goods for sale is impressive. Allison's took over the grocer's shop next door, when that moved across the road and became the Maypole Dairy with Lipton's next door. The Allisons eventually sold out to Woodland's Furnisher's and now a bookmaker occupies the premises. A little further along at 598 Gorton Road was the North Reddish hand laundry with Mrs Wood in charge.

Seven

Special Events

The carnival queen, Fay Kewley (née Aspinall) aged fifteen, on Gorton Road, 1928. Behind Fay are her two heralds, who blew a fanfare on their bugles. The open carriage proceeded along Gorton Road to Broadstone Road, along Levenshulme Road and back via Gorton Road to a field, where the crowning ceremony took place.

A postcard sent during the First World War to soldiers at the front from members of St Elisabeth's church, Christmas 1916. This series of cards was used by many towns with the sender's name printed at the bottom. During the Second World War Belgian refugees came to Reddish and were given shelter in various houses. One Belgian soldier named Vermeulen (aged twenty two), is buried in Willow Grove cemetery in an unmarked grave.

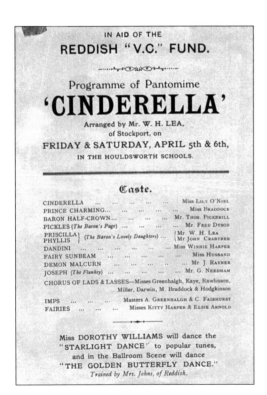

IN AID OF THE
REDDISH "V.C." FUND.

Programme of Pantomime

'CINDERELLA'

Arranged by Mr. W. H. LEA,
of Stockport, on

FRIDAY & SATURDAY, APRIL 5th & 6th,

IN THE HOULDSWORTH SCHOOLS.

Caste.

CINDERELLA	Miss Lily O'Niel
PRINCE CHARMING	Miss Braddock
BARON HALF-CROWN	Mr. Thos. Pickerill
PICKLES (*The Baron's Page*)	Mr. Fred Dyson
PRISCILLA } (*The Baron's Lovely Daughters*) ...	{ Mr. W. H. Lea
PHYLLIS }	{ Mr John Crabtree
DANDINI	Miss Winnie Harper
FAIRY SUNBEAM	Miss Husband
DEMON MALCURN	Mr. J. Rayner
JOSEPH (*The Flunkey*)	Mr. G. Needham

CHORUS OF LADS & LASSES—Misses Greenhalgh, Kaye, Rawlinson, Miller, Darwin, M. Braddock & Hodgkinson

IMPS	Masters A. Greenhalgh & C. Fairhurst
FAIRIES	Misses Kitty Harper & Elsie Arnold

Miss DOROTHY WILLIAMS will dance the "STARLIGHT DANCE" to popular tunes, and in the Ballroom Scene will dance "THE GOLDEN BUTTERFLY DANCE."
Trained by Mrs. Johns, of Reddish.

The cover of a programme for the pantomime *Cinderella*, performed in St Elisabeth's church school during the First World War, *c.* 1917. The money raised went towards the Reddish VC (Victoria Cross) Fund. Soldier Joe Lister of Reddish won the VC for his action in France. During the Boer War a Reddish Relief Fund had been set up and raised money by arranging events such as concerts, for widows and orphans of soldiers killed in the war.

The war memorial to those former pupils of St Elisabeth's Houldsworth day school who were killed during the First World War. The memorial contains seventy four names. Eleven of the eighty two soldiers recruited from Christ Church died in that war and in the Second World War three of the thirty four from Christ Church were lost. Forty three men and two women served in the forces from Greg's mills in the Second World War and three were lost.

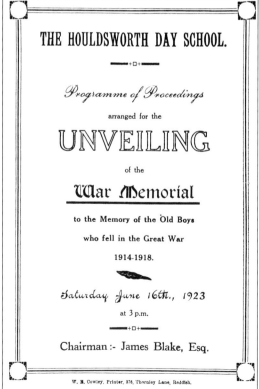

The cover of the programme for the unveiling of the war memorial of St Elisabeth's Houldsworth school, June 1923. Mary Pollitt and George Steele, who were orphaned during the war, unveiled this memorial. An address was given by the chairman, James Blake and the *Last Post* was played with a minute's silence, then the *Reveille* and floral tributes were laid.

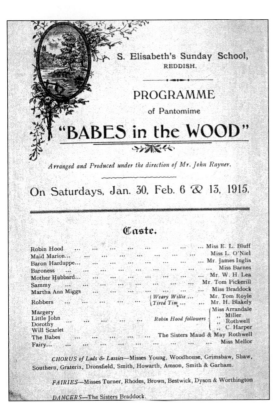

S. Elisabeth's Sunday School,
REDDISH.

PROGRAMME
of Pantomime

"BABES in the WOOD"

Arranged and Produced under the direction of Mr. John Rayner.

On Saturdays, Jan. 30, Feb. 6 & 13, 1915.

Caste.

Robin Hood	... Miss E. L. Bluff
Maid Marion	Miss L. O'Niel
Baron Harduppe	... Mr. James Inglis
Baroness	... Miss Barnes
Mother Hubbard	... Mr. W. H. Lea
Sammy	... Mr. Tom Pickerill
Martha Ann Miggs	... Miss Braddock
Robbers { Weary Willie ...	Mr. Tom Royle
{ Tired Tim ...	Mr. H. Blakely
Margery {	Miss Arrandale
Little John { Robin Hood followers	„ Miller
Dorothy {	„ Rothwell
Will Scarlet {	„ C. Harper
The Babes	The Sisters Maud & May Rothwell
Fairy	... Miss Mellor

CHORUS of *Lads & Lassies*—Misses Young, Woodhouse, Grimshaw, Shaw, Southern, Graterix, Dronsfield, Smith, Howarth, Amson, Smith & Garham.

FAIRIES—Misses Turner, Rhodes, Brown, Bestwick, Dyson & Worthington

DANCERS—The Sisters Braddock.

The cover of the programme for *Babes in the Wood*, staged by St Elisabeth's Sunday school, 1915. The producer was John Rayner. *Dick Whittington* was performed in the following year. They managed to continue performances during both world wars.

Kathleen Dore, who was a government inspector for the production of 'sticky bombs' during the Second World War, *c.* 1943. Kay Bros of Kayborough Works, Reddish, were asked to develop this anti-tank device. Winston Churchill ordered, 'Sticky bomb. Make a million. W.S.C.' The bomb consisted of a glass (later plastic) bulb containing explosives, with a handle and covered in a woollen jacket coated with adhesive. Two and half million were produced.

This derelict shop was once a rest shelter for soldiers wounded during the First World War. There were various shelters, including this one on the approach to Reddish North Station and another opposite, near the junction of Station Road (earlier Sandfold Lane), at 457, Gorton Road, which was converted from a shop. It lies in a row of shops marked by a plaque recording, 'Market Place 1878'. This one later became a greengrocer's shop.

Fay Kewley, carnival queen, 1928. She wore a blue cloak and carried a bouquet of pink roses, her escort consisted of twelve girl guides, six on each side. The carnival was run to raise money for Reddish Crippled Children's Fund and was started in 1921 as a street procession through Windmill Lane and Longford Road. Reddish girls aged between twelve and fifteen were eligible to be chosen to be carnival queen.

Fay Kewley as dowager queen, on the field off Longford Road West, on her way to the throne, 1929. In the year following the one as carnival queen girls became the 'dowager queen' and wore a red cloak. On the left is the queen of 1925, Sylvia Rudd. The first Reddish carnival queen was May Rawlinson in 1921.

Kay Kewley, dowager queen, 1929. She took part in the crowning ceremony and procession with the new carnival queen, who in 1929 was Phyllis Wilson. In the year after being dowager queen girls became the carnival 'Britannia'.

The crowning of Phyllis Wilson as carnival queen seen here with her retinue and helpers on the field off Longford Road West, 1929. Fay Kewley was dowager queen and is at the centre back with Phyllis Wilson on her left and Britannia is two places away on her right. Second from left on the back row is Mrs Ogden who initiated the first carnival. The Mayor of Stockport and his wife are at the back on the right. One boy, at the back, is dressed as an archbishop. On the front row there are flower girls to strew petals, maids-of-honour in the second row and train bearers and heralds.

The first rose queen of St Elisabeth's church, Nora Forshaw, 1907. She was crowned on the school stage but in following years the crowning took place outside in the school yard. Other venues were also used, such as Bradley's Fields at the top of Reddish Vale Road and Thompson's Fields, the rectory lawn and Belle Vue Gardens. The rose queens took part in a procession from Houldsworth Square along Gorton Road to the Bull's Head public house, making various detours on the way.

Joan Dean, the rector's daughter, dowager queen of St Elisabeth's church, rides in an open brougham to the rose queen fête in 1911. The escort was provided by members of the Church Boys' Brigade who carried carbine rifles. Money was collected along the route for charity. Behind the brougham Charles Blore's pawnshop can be seen and the garden wall to the right belongs to the Reddish Conservative Club on Gorton Road (formerly Summerfield House).

May Hamlett being crowned as rose queen of St Elisabeth's church, on Thompson's fields, 1911. Schofield Street is in the background. With her is Joan Dean, the dowager queen.

St Elisabeth's church rose queen fête, 1912. Here the group poses in the rectory grounds with the school in the background. Front row, centre left, are the Revd Rothwell Dean and his wife with Mrs Ferry, the choirmaster's wife. The Revd Dean's daughter, Joan, was rose queen in 1910. Front right sitting on the ground are the 'Little Helpers' wearing gymslips. In the back row centre are Mr Ferry the choirmaster (in straw hat), Miss E. Kemp, Mr Kemp, A. Swale (later Mrs Ridgway) and Arron Arrandale.

John Rayner outside the west door of St Elisabeth's church in the early 1900s. John fulfilled many roles at the church, including organising the Rose Queen fêtes, producing the pantomimes, being superintendent at the Sunday school and leader of the Young Members' Society.

St Elisabeth's church rose queen fête, 1912. Here on the rectory lawn the rose queen, Elsie Partington, and her retinue watch dancers performing. A girls' club met at the Sunday school and among their many activities was dancing.

Marjorie Downham, rose queen of St Elisabeth's church, in procession on Gorton Road near the junction with Betley Road (right), opposite North Reddish Park, in 1913. These houses still exist.

St Elisabeth church's rose queen at her crowning in 1914. That year the queen was Amy Fletcher, the daughter of the People's Warden. The dowager queen was Marjorie Downham. The crowning took place on Thompson's Fields opposite Houldsworth school.

St Elisabeth's rose queen with maids-of-honour, sceptre bearers and retinue in June 1925. The group posed for the photograph inside Houldsworth school after the crowning ceremony. The queen, Jennie Howarth, was the twenty-first Reddish rose queen.

Alice Sunderland, rose queen of St Elisabeth's, photographed in the school yard in the 1940s. She was crowned by the mother of the rector, the Revd T.J. Jeans. Her dowager queen was Peggy Mason.

Sunday evensong at St Elisabeth's church, 1958. After the procession on the Saturday, it was customary for the rose queen and her retinue to attend church. Muriel Rogerson, the rose queen, sits in the front row on the left-hand side and her dowager queen, Dorothy Lewis, is on the right hand side. The fête changed over the years from a one day to a two day event.

Christine Knowles, rose queen of St Elisabeth's church, with her retinue in the school yard in 1959. Her father, Frank Knowles, played a major organising role in the rose queen fêtes and also in local amateur dramatic productions (see p. 112).

The rose queen procession of St Elisabeth's church in the 1950s. Here members of the Church Lads' Brigade march along Gorton Road near Houldsworth Square, with the former police station on the left. Sixth from the left is Frank Knowles with third from the left, Lawrence Young and next to him the drummer Ron Moore.

The Rose queen of St Agnes' church, Joyce Brindley (née Allison), 1958. The procession is seen here near the Reddish Vale public house. The three boys at the front are from the left, A.Gleave and John and Malcolm Buckley.

Joyce Brindley with her attendents outside the Sunday school building just after the crowning in 1958. The ladies-in-waiting, one each side of her, are Patricia Lowndes (left) and Maureen McCormack (right). The maids-of-honour are, back row, left to right: Pat Gandy, Lesley Robinson, C. Jones. The train bearers are: Katherine Plant, Brenda Greenwood, Kathleen McCormack and Glenys Rowley.

Joyce Mellor, rose queen of St Agnes' church, 1959. On the left is Joyce Brindley, now the retiring queen. They are seated on the stage in the Sunday school on Beresford Crescent.

The rose queen procession of St Agnes' church on Beresford Crescent in 1960 and two years after her time as queen Joyce Brindley is now Britannia. She is accompanied by the retiring rosebud queen Kathleen McCormack.

Twenty queens from Reddish and Stockport, lined up for this photograph at Fir Tree Primary school, for an 'at-home' given by Susan Ash, the queen of Fir Tree primary school, 1960. Back row, from left to right: Joyce Brindley, -?-, Joyce Mellor (St Elizabeth's rose queen), Barbara Dean (carnival queen), -?-, -?-, -?-. Front row: Kathleen McCormack (rosebud queen of St Agnes'), -?-, -?-, Susan Ash, Elaine Jones (retiring queen of Fir Tree), Julie Birch, -?-. Mr and Mrs Joyce hosted the reception and social.

A Whit Walk procession in the late 1920s. Here representatives from St Elisabeth's church, assembled under the Mothers' Union banner, join in the hymn singing at Houldsworth Square.

Members of Reddish Congregational church set off for the Whit Walks from their church in Lillian Grove in 1937. First on the left is Edith Duncan.

A Whit Walks procession in the mid 1950s. Here the young members of St Agnes' church walk near their church with, on the left, Miss Burnett, head of the infants at North Reddish Council School.

A Whit Walks procession in the mid 1950s. Young members of St Agnes' church assemble near the church on Gorton Road.

A Whit Walks procession in the early 1960s. The 1st Reddish Brownies are seen carrying their owl and toadstool along Gorton Road. At this point they would have been just passing Allison's hardware shop, opposite the Bull's Head public house (hidden behind the bus).

A Whit Walk procession in the 1960s and here are members of St Agnes' 1st Reddish Brownies. Mrs Rowley, in uniform, is just to the right of the banner and Joyce Brindley leads the group, on the left, behind the banner.

Coronation Day, 2 June 1953. Melbourne Street celebrated the event with a party at which Jean Kewley, daughter of Fay Kewley (see p. 128) was queen for the day. Here she is seated with her retinue in the passageway. They had a party in the top room of the Co-operative shop, the Guild Room, at the top of Ainsdale Grove.

Celebrations in Marland Crescent for the Queen's Silver Jubilee in 1977. Here from left to right are: Elsie Fox, Jayne Mellett, Lil Pegg, Fay Kewley.

Eight
Sports and Leisure

Chorus girls in pantomime at St Elisabeth's church posing outside Houldsworth school where the show was put on, in the 1930s. From the 1890s onwards an annual pantomime was performed at Christmas, usually in Houldsworth school, by members of the Sunday school. The money raised helped to keep the Sunday school running. By 1939 they were calling themselves 'The Amateur Pantomime Company'. In 1970 they were still running but now as 'The Amateur Pantomime & Opera Company'.

HOULDSWORTH CLUB,
REDDISH GREEN.

GRAND PANTOMIME,

"The Enchanted Forest,"

(Written and arranged by G. B. BALL,)

On Saturday, Monday, Tuesday and Wednesday,

JANUARY 25th, 27th, 28th and 29th,

And Saturday, February 1st, 1896

PIANIST - - Mr. C. GOULD.
VIOLIN - - Mr. B. K. GREEN.

(Assisted by Messrs. HEWITT and JEMPHSON)
(Mandoline and Banjo).

Scenery specially painted for this Pantomime by G. B. BALL.

Costumes by HUME, of 90, Oxford Road, Manchester.

Manager, Mr. G. B. BALL.

Doors open at 7; commence at 7-30.

WILLIAM KEMP, Printer, Hyde Road, Ardwick.

The programme cover for the pantomime *The Enchanted Forest* performed at the Houldsworth working men's club, 1896. This was probably the first pantomime to be staged at the club by members of St Elisabeth's Sunday school. They created a repertoire of pantomimes, performing *Dick Whittington* in 1905, 1908 and 1916 and *Babes in the Wood* in 1907, 1915 and 1929.

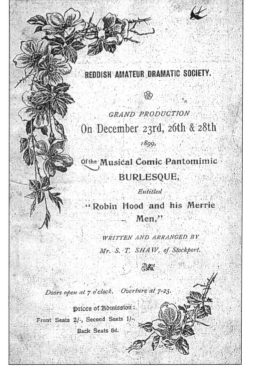

REDDISH AMATEUR DRAMATIC SOCIETY.

GRAND PRODUCTION
On December 23rd, 26th & 28th
1899,

Of the Musical Comic Pantomimic
BURLESQUE,

Entitled

"Robin Hood and his Merrie Men,"

WRITTEN AND ARRANGED BY
Mr. S. T. SHAW, of Stockport.

Doors open at 7 o'clock. Overture at 7-25.

Prices of Admission :
Front Seats 2/-, Second Seats 1/-,
Back Seats 6d.

The programme cover for the pantomime *Robin Hood and His Merrie Men*, performed by the Reddish Amateur Dramatic Society, who were members of St Elisabeth's church, in 1899. This group put on a variety of dramatic entertainments from the 1890s onwards, including *East Lynne* in 1894 and *The Spark of Hatred* in 1900.

The cast of a pantomime performed by members of St Elisabeth's church in the 1920s. They are seen here posing outside the front entrance of Houldsworth school. The pantomime is thought to have been *Robinson Crusoe*.

The programme cover for a performance of *Leah* by members of St Elisabeth's church in 1895. The proceeds of the event went towards providing the Church Lads' Brigade with rifles and a brass band. The Boer wars were in progress and the Church Lads' Brigade drilled and practised with weapons during this and the First World War.

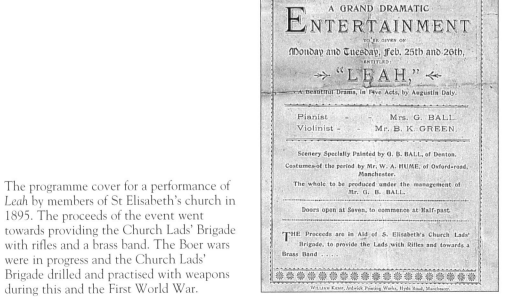

The cast of the pantomime *Puss in Boots* performed by members of St Elisabeth's church, *c.* 1939. The producer was Mr J.C. Kemp. On the second row from the front, first right is Norah Knowles and second right is Frank Knowles. Frank performed in and produced these plays from 1956 until 1980 and was well known for organising rose queen fêtes at St Elisabeth's. He and his wife were the last tenants to live at The Priory (see p. 37).

Members of St Elisabeth's church Sunday school in fancy dress in the 1930s.

Members of St Elisabeth's church pantomime group on a ramble in the Goyt valley, in around 1951. This ramble was an annual event for all ages to attend.

Members of a pantomime cast at St Elisabeth's church enjoying tea together after a dress rehearsal in the early 1950s. They held the dress rehearsal and then, after tea, performed the first public show in Houldsworth school. That year it was *Little Bo Peep*.

The cast of the farce *The Time of Your Life*, performed by SARADS (St Agnes' (Reddish) Amateur Dramatic Society) in 1966. Seated first right is Marion Walton, who played Grandma Pickering. The rector was president of the society.

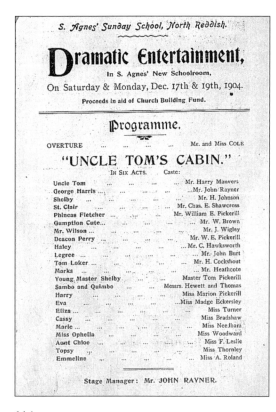

The programme cover for the performance of *Uncle Tom's Cabin* by members of St Agnes' Sunday school in 1904. This was performed in the newly opened Sunday school room, the money raised going towards the church building fund. First a mission room and then the mission church were used until the permanent church was erected in 1908. The producer, John Rayner, was a well-known figure in Reddish, producing plays for St Elisabeth's, as well as St Agnes', and for being an organiser of rose queen fetes at St Elisabeth's (see p. 97).

A troupe of Morris dancers trained by John Rayner and Arron Arrandale in the yard of Houldsworth school, in around 1912, when Arron was caretaker of the day school. The canvas backdrop was to stop people peeping in for a free show. The chimney belonged to the Phoenix chemical works of Charles Lowe at the north end of Houldsworth Street. Established in 1867 at the end of Priory Lane by the canal, they produced oils and synthetic resins, as well as phenol (carbolic acid). The tall stills used in the production were visible for miles around. By 1975 new housing covered the factory site.

An improvised bagpipe band on Houldsworth Square, by the Houldsworth Hotel, in July 1952. The band was supporting the dancers of Mrs Mason's dancing school at the rose queen fête.

Reddish Prize Band, 1915. The band was formed from members of St Elisabeth's church Lads' Brigade in 1897. They played at local festivals and carnivals and annually at midnight in Houldsworth Square on New Year's Eve.

Members of St Elisabeth's church Lads' Brigade setting out from church for a Whit Walk in the late 1950s. At the front is Lawrence Young with Ronnie Moore on the left. Behind them is the mill of the Reddish Spinning Company on Houldsworth Street.

This is an early example of flash light photography from the late 1890s. Members of St Elisabeth's Lads' Club pose in their clubroom in Schofield Street. Note the fashion for Eton collars and billiards which was popular then. In 1907 their meeting place was in the Yew Tree Inn where they used the snug as an office, the taproom for billiards, the kitchen for recreation, the bar parlour for reading and upstairs for the band, stores and offices.

Reddish Church Lads' Brigade at camp at Prestatyn, *c.* 1906. Captain Oldfield is seated centre with the Revd Paul Bull behind him wearing a white cap. The curate or rector was usually the chaplain. The company had about seventy members at this time. Their sporting activities included cricket and drilling and by 1910 the company had a gymnastics team.

The old Thatched tavern on Stanhope Street (originally John Street), lying by the canal and railway, *c.* 1882. The main way to the station once ran in front of the inn. The woman on the left is Mrs Knight and her husband, Alfred, the licensee, is standing fourth from the right wearing a white apron. The men in white aprons are probably cellarmen. The rest are stonemasons and bricklayers, about to build the replacement inn. The row of houses next door was known as the 'prison houses', as they were built of bricks from Belle Vue Prison.

The Houldsworth Arms or Hotel in Houldsworth Square in the late 1940s. On the left is Reddish Road and on the right Broadstone Road. This photograph was taken after a facelift, when the pub received a facing of tiles. Note that the square was still cobbled and shows tramlines. On the right of the pub, on Broadstone Road, is the Co-operative stores of Stockport Industrial and Equitable Society.

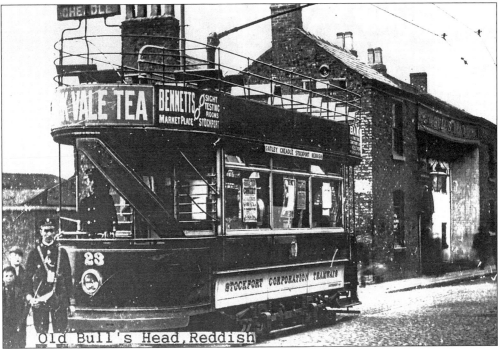

The tramcar of the Stockport Corporation Tramways Co. at the Bull's Head public house on Gorton Road, c. 1905. This pub became the terminus, as it lay near the borders between Reddish, Denton and Gorton, between Stockport and Manchester City. Manchester City Corporation trams took over along Reddish Lane. The first Bull's Head, where bull baiting took place until 1829, was demolished in 1906 and had its name board strung across the entrance to its yard.

119

Some early members of the North Reddish Working Men's Club on Midland Road, in around 1911. The founding president was Mr Malyran with Mr Ironfield, vice-president. The first chairman was Mr Travis and the secretary Mr Prior. The original membership of 20 had grown to over 1,300 by the time of the club's Golden Jubilee in 1985. The club members played various indoor sports such as snooker and darts and outdoor ones such as football and crown bowls. A ladies' section organised concerts and raised money for the club.

The original club building of the North Reddish Working Men's Club in around 1911, when the club set up in this small house on Hobson Street with twenty members. By 1913 they owned a building on Midland Road, adding an army hut to the accommodation in 1922. The present clubhouse was erected in 1935 and was extended in 1968 providing living accommodation for the steward's family. A games room was added in 1980. An upstairs dance hall became a children's nursery during the Second World War and then the club's concert hall.

Advertisements for the Bijou and Reddish Picture Hall cinemas. The latter is from around 1913. The Bijou was in Priory Lane and operated from 1916 until 1939, the building surviving until 1966. The cinema had its own football and athletics teams and generated its own electricity. The Reddish Picture Hall, seating 650, opened on Gorton Road near the Bull's Head in 1913, became the Pavilion in 1917 and then the Embassy in 1932. The Embassy burned down in 1933 and was replaced in 1934 by the Rota in Thornley Lane, on the borders of Denton and Reddish. The cinema was designed by Henry Elder, seated 1,206 people and operated until 1959. The building was demolished in the 1960s.

The bingo hall on Gorton Road (Priory Lane on the left) in 1995. This building began life as the County cinema, later becaming the Essoldo, and operated from 1938 until 1969 when it became the bingo hall, now demolished. The County was opened by Frank Donaldson who also owned the Bijou. The Bijou was a tin cinema and was also known as the 'Bug Hut'. When it rained the noise on the corrugated iron roof was sometimes so loud that it drowned out the sound of the film. Entrance to it was one penny and included a free comic.

The club house of Reddish Vale Golf Club is situated at the end of Southcliffe Road. This stone-built house began life as a private house called Southcliff with spacious grounds (see p. 49). The golf course was laid out in 1912 in its grounds stretching down to the River Tame with the first six holes lying on the Lancashire side of the river and the rest on the Cheshire side. The golf architect, Dr Alister MacKenzie, was brought in to tame the ravines, swamps, quagmires and sandy subsoil.

Albert Modest St Chevalier, 1930. The son of Charles St Chevalier, the professional golfer at Reddish Vale from 1921 until 1938/9, he assisted his father at Reddish Vale from 1922. Albert, who became the professional at Romiley from 1963 until 1977, designed a new type of putter and held the world record for number of holes-in-one achieved – thirty one. Charles was the professional at Romiley between 1909 and 1921 and at Heaton Moor from 1940 -1970. The family originated from the Channel Isles.

The club house of Houldsworth Golf Club, prior to demolition, 1992. This building was previously Wingate (or Wyngate) House, built by Mr Hammond, father of Robert Hammond of the print works at Reddish Vale. He built the nearby print works but later moved to the larger premises in the vale. The house had also been rectory for St Elisabeth's church and was later a farm. The golf club added the extension to the house, which was demolished to make way for housing. A new club house was opened in 1993.

The Eighteenth hole of Houldsworth golf course, 1935. It was proposed to construct a golf club here in 1910 and 120 people subscribed to it each paying an entrance fee of £1 1s 0d. Sir William Houldsworth was patron and Cllr John Harrop was president. A silver medallion was presented by Sir William as an annual prize. The club is situated on the boundary of Levenshulme and Reddish on Longford Road West, adjoining Pink Bank Lane. The eighteen hole course was eventually bought by the club in 1922.

The football team of Houldsworth school in 1915, after receiving the Stockport cup which they won a record number of times. On the right is Arron Arrandale, coach and school caretaker and second from the left at the front is Cllr Harold Kemp. First on the left at the back is Frank Knowles.

A football team on the Longford Road West ground a couple of years before they formed officially as Reddish Park Albion, in the 1930s. Third from the right, middle row is Harold Kewley and in the front row, second from right, is John Aspinall and fourth Jack Aspinall. They went on to win the cup.

Reddish Park Albions football team in the year they won the cup, thought to be 1933. Second from the left, middle row is Harold Kewley. All the local schools and churches had football teams and others included Reddish United, Reddish Celtic, Craven's, Hornsby's and Barlow Fold Association.

North Reddish school football team in the year they won the school shield, sometime in the late 1920s. They played on the Longford Road West ground. In the back row, second from left, is Mr Sheldon, fourth is Harold Kewley and eighth is Bill Kewley. In the front row, first from right, is John Aspinall.

St Elisabeth's football team at South Reddish park in the late 1940s.

Frank Aspinall (1908-1985) who devoted many of his seventy seven years to promoting football in Reddish. Frank was a chimney sweep and gardener but was best known as 'Mr Football'. He was the manager for Westbourne Rangers (Reddish & District Junior League) and was a scout for Stockport County for many years. For a time Frank managed six teams at once, including Vale Road Juniors from 1941-7.

St Elisabeth's church choir boys cricket club, 1915. In the back row is the curate who ran this club. In a 1907 match between the parish church choir Cantoris and Decani the the Cantoris team won by thirty runs. The umpires were Houldsworth school head, Mr Broadbent, and the bass singer in the choir, Mr W. Lea. Cricket teams were put up by the churches, schools, streets and companies and included such names such as Daisy Fields, Barlow Lane, Little Ireland, South Reddish, North Reddish, Reddish and Spencer/Salisbury Streets.

Taking a break on the allotments behind Harcourt Street in the 1920s. There were three greenhouses on the allotments and a duck pond. The Aspinalls, who lived on Harcourt Street, were keen gardeners. On the right are Walter and Edith Grantham (née Aspinall) and on the left are her parents, John and Annie Aspinall. Walter's parents were caretakers at All Saints' church, Gorton. There were more allotments along the canal and many nurseries. One nurseyman, B.W. Witham, developed and recorded a new variety of apple, the Lord Derby, in 1862.

Fay Kewley sits with her daughter Jean in their home in Melbourne Street in the early 1950s. In the background is their new television set, not something to be found in every home at that time. Queen Elizabeth's Coronation in 1953 encouraged many people to get a set to view the event. Fay has lived at this house for over sixty years.

Harold Kewley, aged about twelve, playing the violin in around 1910. Harold was a good violinist, accompanying his stepmother, who played the piano. Making music together was a family pastime in the days before television. Harold's family had a coal merchants business near Reddish station.